Pastel Punch

Stevan

40 Pastel Paintings On Paper

Cover: Shock and Awe

Copyright © 2012

Stevan CS

S

Dreaming

S

Hungry

S

Mr. Green

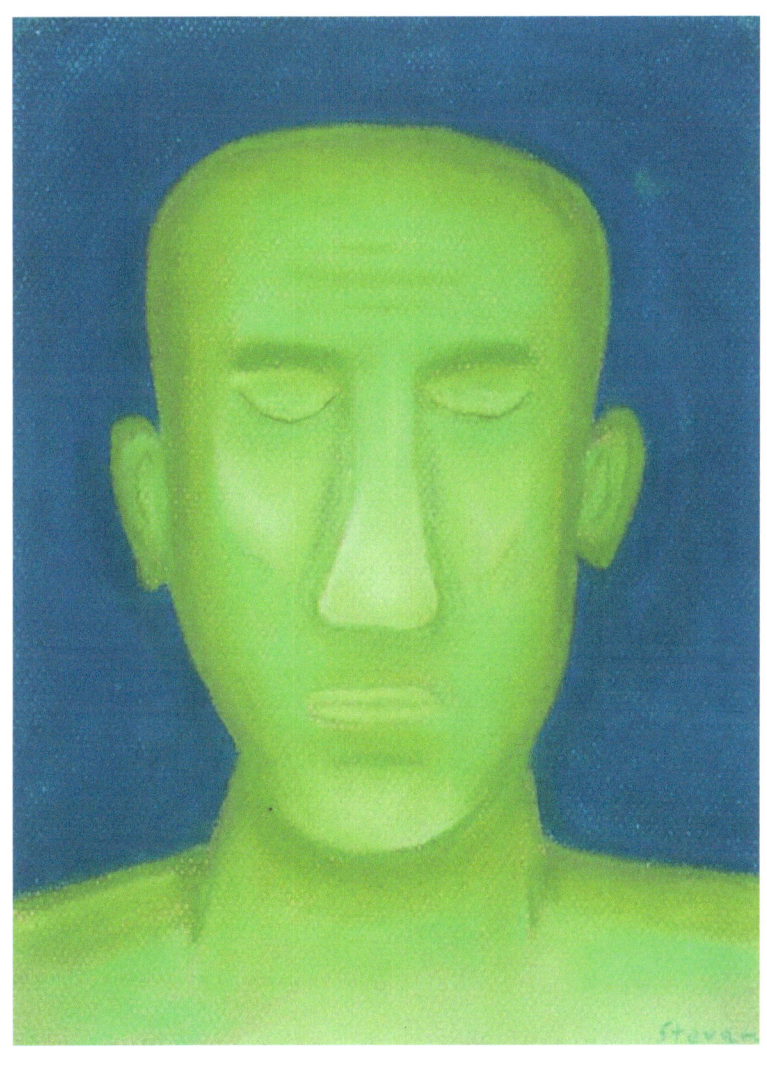

S

Hermaphrodite

S

Controversy

S

Joe Normal

S

Mt. Olympus

S

The Kiss

S

The Deep

S

Coming Home

S

Beautiful Balloon

S

Lionman

S

Reality

S

Determined

S

Seagull View

S

Harlequin

S

Progress

S

Astonished

S

Water

S

Nude

S

Foreign Land

S

Little Boy Blue

S

Pitcher

S

New Day

S

Ovum

S

Death Mask

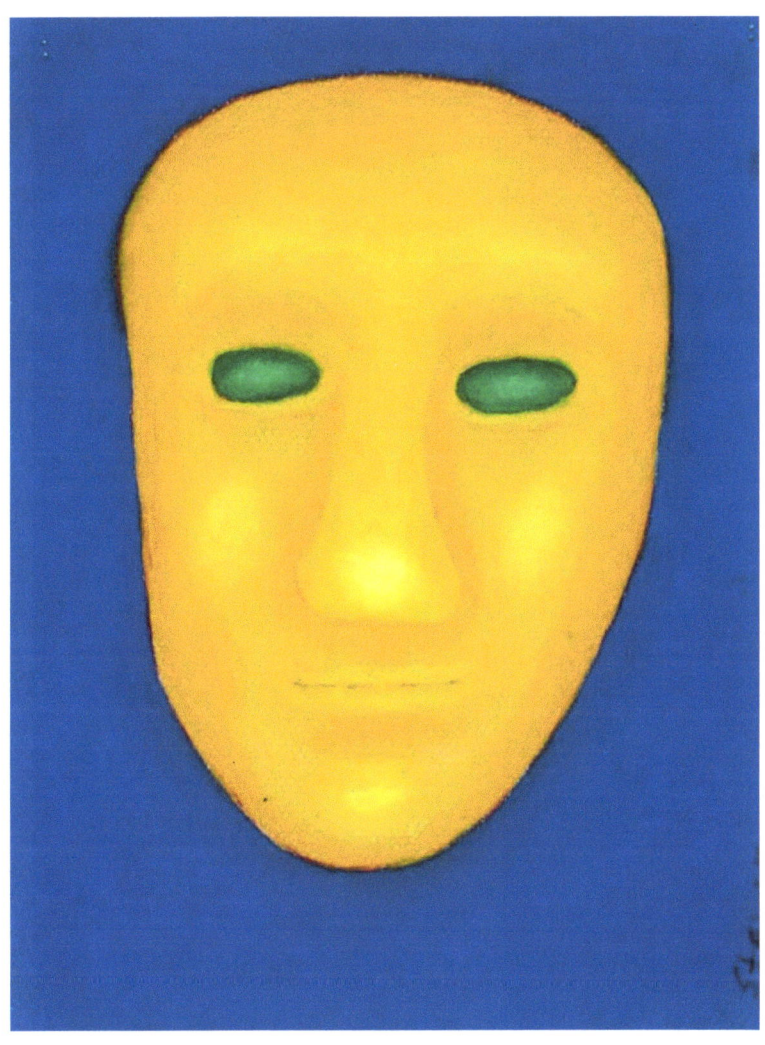

S

Liquid

S

Office Manager

S

Pussywillow

S

Moonlight

S

Love

S

Life and Death

S

Time

S

Black Hole

S

Cold Landscape

S

Simba

S

Floppy

S

Masquerade

S

Smile

www.ingramcontent.com/pod-product-compliance
Lightning Source LLC
Chambersburg PA
CBHW041103180526
45172CB00001B/84